MIRAGE OF THE MIRROR

MIRAGE OF THE MIRROR

SAMINA **SAIFEE**

PARTRIDGE
A Penguin Random House Company

ISBN:	Hardcover	978-1-4828-3953-1
	Softcover	978-1-4828-3954-8
	eBook	978-1-4828-3952-4

To order additional copies of this book, contact
Partridge India
000 800 10062 62
orders.india@partridgepublishing.com

www.partridgepublishing.com/india

Contents

Dedication

FATHER:
SHABBIR SHAMSHUDDIN SAIFEE.

MOTHER:
BILKIS SHABBIR SAIFEE.

THE AUTHOR DECLARES THE CREDIT FOR HER PASSIONATE WRITING WHICH WAS DISCOVERED WAS THROUGH HER SPECIAL FRIEND, JOAN RODRIGUES.

SHE IS THANKFUL TO HER DEAR ONE MUSTAFA (NAUSHAD) KHUMRI FOR HIS HARD EFFORTS TO MAKE THIS BOOK A GREAT SUCCESS.

Acknowledgements

Here's a confession:

A heartfelt thanks to all the assistants and participants who made this dream come true. Your inspiring heroic efforts and your courage in confronting the obstacles and ordeals helped me to make these a great outcome.

The book you hold in your hands has been published into its present shape by the Publishing Consultant Maveric Pana who prompted me with this idea to issue it successfully. We have never met but our way of interacting through phone and through exchange of emails almost makes me feel the sense of genuine human touch.

I'd like to thank my dear one Naushad (Mustafa) Khumri who ultimately made this publishing workout through his great effort and made sure that this book reaches to every reader all over the world.

Thankyou, for being who you truly are as a role model for the vision of this great book that the world so desperately needs.

The exclusive sketches which you see on it's pages is all contributed by the artistic and creative work due which I am thankful to my distant friend Mr.Deva Prasad.

I am thankful to God for blessing me with this book to get published and issued and to every reader who has this book in their hands.

POEMS

IN SEARCH OF LOVE.

IN SEARCH OF LOVE........

IN THE MIDDLE OF THE NIGHT
I WAS CAUGHT UNAWARE
THAT FORTY WINKS WHICH I COULD NOT CATCH,

AS A JILTED LOVER
I FOUGHT MY BATTLE
ONLY TO SEE MYSELF MUCH MORE IN UTTER DESPAIR,

I LOST MY LOVE
MY LOVE HAD FORGONE ME
WITH THIS DEEP SOLITARINESS
I HOPE MY LIFE WOULD NOT BE A MESS,

I SEEK LOVE IN THE NAME OF MY SOUL-MATE
BUT MY BELOVED CEASED TO EXIST
IN MY LIFE OF WORLDLY AFFAIRS,

DUE TO HIS LOVE TOWARDS ME OR
DUE TO HIS HATRED,
WITH NO REASONS TO BELIEVE
I WAS LOST IN THE WORLD
WHICH WAS HARD TO PERCEIVE
I BECAME SEEKING HIM
IN SEARCH OF HIS LOVE ETERNALLY...........

IT IS NOT MUCH TO WIN
NOT MUCH TO LOSE,
MY BELOVED CONFESSED TO ME
HE BECAME VICTIM OF HIS OWN CIRCUMSTANCE,

WHEREAS I CREATED CHAOS IN MY LIFE
WHEN HE TURNED AWAY AT VERY FIRST INSTANCE,
NOW TO KEEP FORLORN HOPE AND
SEE WHAT LUCK HAS IN STORE
I CRIED OUT A RIVER
ONLY FOR GETTING MYSELF CONSOLED,

THIS ENDLESS SEARCH FOR LOVE HAS NOW COME TO HALT
AS THE REASON WHOM I LOVED
EXISTS IN MY VIVID MEMORIES WITHOUT MY FAULT,

AS LIFE HAS A REASON TO LIVE WITH
HERE I COME TO LIVE AND SUBMIT IT
WITH NO PURPOSE TO SERVE
MY REAL LOVE.

I CAN FEEL HIS MESMERIZED EYES
I CAN FEEL HIS SOUL
BUT MY LOVE DOES NOT KNOW
WHERE I AM WITH THIS THOUGHT.

WITH THIS CONQUERENCE OF PAIN
I CEASE TO LOVE ANYONE I GAIN.
HOPING MY LOVE TO COME BACK
BEFORE MY LIFE WOULD END.

THOSE BLACKOUT DAYS BACK IN KASHMIR.

THOSE BLACKOUT DAYS........ BACK IN KASHMIR

I WAS MAROONED IN A DESERTED LIFE OF GLOOMY LAND
IN MY HEART I HELD TRUE LOVE
WHICH I WASN'T ABLE TO PURSUE TILL THE END,

LIFE IS IN PAIN INDEED
WITHOUT MY LOVE WHO HAD TO TURN APART
WHEN I WAS UTMOST IN HIS NEED,

IN HIS VIVID MEMORIES I SURVIVE
WITH THIS HEARTFELT LOVE I RESORT TO LIVE MY LIFE,

BUT MY LOVE WAS SO IDEAL AND SO UNIQUE
HE WAS SO HEAVENLY AND COSMIC
THAT I REGRET MY SINS OF INTIMACY
WHICH APPEALED AT THE BACK OF MY MIND TO FANCY,

THERE WERE BLACKOUT DAYS BACK THERE IN KASHMIR
MY HEAVENLY LOVE WANDERED HERE AND THERE
WITHOUT MY SPIRIT OF LIFE TO CHEER,

WHEN I WAS YET TO BE IN LIMELIGHT
HE WAS FAST ASLEEP THERE IN DARKEST NIGHT [BLACKOUT DAYS OF KASHMIR]
HE WAS UNAWARE HOW MUCH HIS BELOVED CARE
COUNTING THOSE DAYS OF BLACKOUT WHICH I CANNOT SHARE
I SURVIVED IN THE LIGHT OF HOPE
ONE DAY MY SOUL-SEEKER WILL COME UP TO COPE ALL SADNESS I SOB,

HE WILL CUDDLE ME
HE WILL CARESS ME
LIKE AN INFANT
WHO IS DEADLY STILL-BORN,

THE VERY SIGHT OF HIM
AT EVERY PASSING THOUGHT
I THINK OF MYSELF THAT
I CANNOT SURVIVE AS
WITHOUT HIM I AM ALMOST LOST,

THERE WAS BLACKOUT IN THE WORLD'S MOST HEAVENLY PLACE [KASHMIR]
AND I AM YET TO DISCOVER A SPOTLIGHT
FOR MY LOVE ON THIS EARTHLY MESS [WORLD].

CALL ME! COME BACK!
THIS CAN BE THE ONLY POSSIBLE NOTE
WHICH I COULD LEAVE HIM AND NEVER REPLACE....
YOU NEVER GONNA SEE ME SUFFER LIKE THIS IN UTMOST DESPAIR
AM WAITING WITH THIS PERIOD OF MY TEAR-SHEDDING DAYS
HOPING THIS BLACKOUT WILL SOON TURN UP TO HAVE BRIGHT RAYS,

I DO NOT NEED TO REACH PARADISE
AS HEAVENLY LOVE I SAW DEEP IN HIS EYES,
AS MUCH DEEP AS THE RIVER PASSES BY,

ALL BY THE WILL OF ALMIGHTY
TIME WILL TELL
MY FORTUNE HAS A FORECAST
TO WHICH EVEN VOODOO CANNOT CAST A MAGICAL SPELL.

SO MUCH TO WRITE
SO MUCH TO SAY
THAT I DISCLOSED MY LAST CHAPTER OF WAITING LESSONS
AS TIME HAS TOLD ME TO KEEP SOME MORE PATIENCE
YES, TIME IS TESTING MY OWN PATIENCE WHICH I HAVEN'T LOST
SOMEONE WILL KNOCK MY DOOR
FOR HEAVENLY ABODE IN ETERNAL ALMOST.

THIS LIBERTY OF LOVE
NEITHER FREEDOM
NOR ARREST
MAY MY LOVE WILL COME BACK
LEAVING ENTIRE EARTH TO REST.

THIS MOMENT OF DANCE
NEITHER STILL
NOR MOVEMENT
MAY MY LOVE WILL COME AHEAD
WHEN I MAKE MY FORTUNE
WITH MY SOUL RUNNING STILL AND STAGNATE.

THESE BLACKOUT DAYS OF KASHMIR
HAS SET SOME RAYS OF HOPE AND
SOME CLOUDS TO FLOAT
OH GOD! I SWEAR
ENTIRE WORLD SOUNDS TO ME LIKE A HELL
LET HEAVEN NOT FALL
HOPE NOT THE HELL
YET, ALL IS WELL
ALL IS WELL!!!

SIGNATURE-SIGNATURE

SIGNATURE-SIGNATURE
YOU WILL NEVER KNOW IT'S NATURE,
SO MANY WAYS TO SIGN,
GOES UNDEFINE
THE WORDS OF EVERY LINE,
SO DEFINITE AND FINE
SIGNATURE-SIGNATURE................

WE SIGN ALL PAPERS
WE ARE ONLY IT'S MAKERS
FOR BIRTH TO TAKE PLACE
FOR DEATH CERTIFICATES
FOR MARRIAGE AND DIVORCE
WHICH CANNOT BE FORCED
SIGNATURE-SIGNATURE...............

SO HELPLESS IS A MAN
WITHOUT SIGNING HE CANNOT CHANGE,
FOR HIS DESTINY AND FAME
SIGNATURE IS THE ONLY GAME
SIGNATURE-SIGNATURE..................

WHENEVER COURT JUSTIFIES
AND ITS DECISION JURY DECIDES
SIGNATURE IS THE ONLY WAY
VICTIM'S FUTURE IT CAN PLAY
SIGNATURE-SIGNATURE................

SIGNATURE IS EVERYTHING
IT IS END TO THIS WORLD
WHEN WE ARE KEEN
IT'S VALUE IS SO INDEFINITE AND PRECISE
LIFE'S COMPLICATIONS ARE SOLVED WITH IT
WHEN WE DECIDE
SIGNATURE-SIGNATURE...................

SO SIGN, SIGN AND SIGN
GO UNDEFINED
BE VERY GENEROUS AND KIND
FOR HUMAN-BEINGS TO EXIST ON THIS LAND
SIGNATURE EVERYTIME HAS TO BE CLAIMED
YET, NO ONE CAN BE BLAMED!!!

IN THE NIGHTS OF TERROR WHEN THE LOVE OPERATES

UNDER PLEASURE AND PAIN,
UNDER PLEASURE, PAIN LIES.

UNDER TERROR AND PAIN,
UNDER TERROR, PAIN LIES.

WHEN YOU FIGHT A TERROR
YOU DISCOVER A KIND OF ERROR,
WHEN YOUR LOVE SHOWS IMPERFECTION
WHEN YOUR BELOVED IS YOUR NATION,
TO HOLD YOU TIGHT IN THE FIGHT OF GETTING AFFECTION
YOU REGRET TO LOVE THE ONE
WHO DOESN'T SHOW COURAGE OF CONVICTION,

IN THE NAME OF LOVE WHEN TERROR OPERATES
TO USE YOU AS A MISSION
WHICH HAS A RULE NOT TO COOPERATE,
WHEN THE IMAGE OF MIRROR LIES TO YOU
AND YOU LIE TO YOURSELF,
YOU HATE TO WANDER IN LOVE BLINDLY
IN THE WORLD OF ATROCITIES SO KINDLY,
WHEN YOU LOVE SOMEONE WHOLEHEARTEDLY IN PAIN
AND HIS MOTIVE IS TO RULE YOUR MIND, SLAIN YOU AND GAIN,

THE VICTORY OF HIS VIRTUOUS LIFE IS LOST
HE KISSES THE DUST AND DEATH FOLLOWS HIM ALMOST,
THE SHADOW OF HIM PREVAILS AND

HE FOLLOWS DARKNESS
IN THE PURSUIT OF LIFE
TO DIG HIS OWN GRAVE
IN THE WAKE OF A NIGHT MARE,

WHEN THE RELIGION OF LOVE
TOWARDS HUMANITY BECOMES HATRED
IT'S WORSHIPPING OF DEVIL
IS TO INHUMANLY GET WICKED,
WHEN YOUR LOVE IS WORSHIP INDEED
TO BETRAY SOMEONE BECOMES A CURSE
WHICH ISN'T COUNTED IN HEAVEN AS A GOOD DEED,

WHEN A MAN LOVES A TERROR AND SHOWS HATRED
OPERATES INFIDELITY AND CAUSES BETRAY
DENYING LOVE WHICH WAS SO PURE AND SO SACRED
HE KILLS HIS OWN CONSCIENCE WITHOUT GOD'S FEAR,
AT THE COST OF PATRIOTISM
IT IS A DEVIL WORSHIP AND
AN ACT OF SHEER DIABOLISM,

TO LIFT THE VEIL OF PRIDE AND PREJUDICE
HE LOVED HIS BELOVED IN HIS NATION'S NUDE EYES,
FOR THE RELIGIOUS DISPARITIES PREVAILING IN HIS MIND
HE BREAKS THE TRUST OF HIS BELOVED NATION
FROM WHOM HE CANNOT REVEAL THE TRUTH NOR CAN HE HIDE,

THE ETERNAL LIFE WHICH HE LEAD
TO LIVE ON EARTH
BECOMES DISGUST AND
BRINGS GOD'S WRATH,
WITH DIVINE LOVE

BESTOWED UPON HIM
NEITHER IN HEAVEN
NOR IN HELL ...

HE WILL MERGE WITH THE BLUE SKY
DEPRIVED OF BOUNTIES.

WHICH HE FAILED TO SEEK
AND SEARCH IN HIS BELOVED'S HEART ANYMORE INDEED.

A MERE MIRROR-EFFECT.

A MERE MIRROR-EFFECT

MIRROR MIRROR ON THE WALL!
SAY;
WHO IS THE MANTRI-MINISTER OF THE WORLD?
"YOU MAN" (THE POOR INDIAN'S POLITICAL DON)
IT GOES LIKE THAT IN A FAIRY TALE
THE WORLD OF IMAGINATION... WOW!
WE THE MINISTERS
EITHER MARATHI MANOOS OR BIHARI BABUS
AND YOU THAT POOR PRAJA
I RULE OVER YOU!
YOU SELECT ME AND I GET MY WAY
TO ELECT MYSELF
HA...HA...HA!
SOUNDS GREAT... NA?
A PERILOUS PARADISE
ON EARTH
THAT IS OUR VERY OWN NATION, INDIA
JAI BHARAT!!!

MIND YOU
YOU POOR INDIANS
WE ARE AMERICANS (INTERNATIONALLY SPEAKING)
YOU KNOW WHAT I MEAN.
WE ARE ADVANCED
TECHNOLOGICALLY SPEAKING
WELL..... ECONOMICALLY...
OH YES!
WE MEAN TO CROWN OURSELVES

THAT DOLLARS WE EARN AND YEARN
OVER THE YEARS WE SPENT
YOU HAVE NOTHING,
AS INDIANS ARE RICH IN CULTURE
IRONICALLY SPEAKING,
LET'S DEFEND OURSELVES
WITH NO DEFINITIONS
WE DO RESEARCH
WE THE CREATORS
AS AMERICANS
AND YOU COPY-CATS
JUST DO MERE IMITATION
YOU HAVE NO PLACE FOR INNOVATION
WITH NEW FUNDAMENTAL OPINION
YOU CANNOT EVEN FIGHT TERRORISM
AS WE SUPPLY
ARMS AND AMMUNITION
DISCREETFULLY,
HUSH.......
NO ONE SHOULD KNOW
EXCEPT WIKILEAKS.
WHENEVER IT IS YET TO GET DISCLOSED
OPEN YOUR EYES SEE THE WORLD
OUR UNIVERSE IS NOT SUCH A SMALL MATTER
BUT WE HAVE SEARCHED THE WORLD
THE WAY AMERIGO VES PUSI
FOUND OUR NATION
"AMERICA"...
CHILL!!!
FURTHER MORE WE GOT EXPLORED AND KILLED
INDIANS THINK WE ARE ACHIEVERS

OF WHAT WE WANT BUT
THE FACT IS WE ACHIEVED IT
AT THE COST OF
KILLING OUR OWN CONSCIENCE
IF YOU ARE INDIANS
SORRY!!!
PACK YOUR PASSPORT
YOU ARE NOT OURS AND
WE ARE NOT YOURS
SEE WHAT YOU HAVE AND SEE WHAT WE GET
DOLLARS AND DOLLARS TO SPEND ON DRUGS
KILLING OUR LIFE-TIME
JUST FOR SAKE OF
THOSE PLEASURE SEEKING
TEMPORAL MOMENTS
LIKE MICHAEL JACKSONS
DREADFUL DEATH
WE ARE MISERABLE ON WHAT WE GET
WE ARE POOR INDEED
HOPE! YOU ARE RICH
OH!......FORGET THE DEAL
WHO IS POOR AND WHO IS RICH
WE ARE NOT KIDS
IT SEEMS LIKE
A FULCRUM OF SEE-SAW IN A SMALL GARDEN
INDIANS AND AMERICANS
THOSE RACES AND FACES
WE HAVE MONEY BUT NO TIME
WHEREAS YOU HAVE THE QUALITY OF LIFE
STRETCHED ENOUGH
TO KEEP YOURSELF HAPPILY ALIVE

NO DISCRIMINATION
TO STAY UNITED
IS OUR UTMOST MISSION
BESIDES VESTED INTEREST
PEOPLE OF OUR NATION
LISTEN! NO MORE EMOTIONS TO FUEL
JUST STOP
DIVIDE-AND-RULE.

REMEMBER "EX" FACTOR?

REMEMBER THE FACTOR "EX"
"EX" WAS DRAWN FROM EXPERIMENTATION OF OUR EXORBITANT EXTRAORDINARY LIFE.

FOR THE HECK OF NUPTIAL TIES
"EX'' WAS THE FACTOR WE ALWAYS CRIED!

IT WAS OUR EX WHO MADE US SENSUALISE INTIMACY IS SAFE
UNDER CONVENTIONAL OR SAY MODEST WAY
"EX'' HAS STAMPED STIGMA ON OUR EARTHLY STAY.

SO UNHUMANLY AND SO UNPURE
THE EFFECT WAS LEFT UN-OBSCURED
WHO THE HELL IS MR. EX?

THE ONE WHO JUST CRAVED FOR MATE
LUSTFULLY AND WITHOUT LOTS OF LOVE HE MANAGED
TO GET OUT OF OUR FRAGILE LIFE CLEARLY UNTAXED

TO CELEBRATE AND CHERISH THOSE TEMPORAL MOMENTS
WOULD BRING US BACK WITH HIS ASH
NO SHARING, NO CARING, NO CUDDLING
AND NO NOTHING WILL HOLD US BACK

IT WAS JUST A BIG MISTAKE!
EXCUSE ME! MR. "EX"
NO EXCUSE TO GIVE,
TO BE PLAYED
YOU MADE A WOMAN EMOTIONALLY SLAYED

SHE WAS DRIVEN OUT OF YOUR INSIGNIFICANT FACTUAL FORCE
AND LED HERSELF FREE ENOUGH TO FULFILL HER LIFE, FLY AND FLOAT

NO MATTER WHEREVER SHE GOES
MR. "EX" DO NOT FOLLOW MA'M THOUGH, LIKE A SHADOW
YOU ARE "EX" AND NOT THE MIRROR IMAGE.
BEFORE YOU TRY TO MOVE TOWARDS HER OR ANYONE ELSE.
YOU WILL REGRET CREATING THE EARTH'S BIGGEST MESS,

THAT'S MR. "EX"
BETTER DON'T TRY TO CHASE!
LEAVE HER AND LET HER LEAVE YOU AT THIS PHASE.

IS NEWS MUSE?

IS NEWS MUSE?

IN THESE DAY AND AGE
NEWS IS A MUSE
SO DON'T GET AMUSED,

WHAT'S IN NEWS
IS IT'S WORLDLY REVIEWS,
LOOKING AT OUR HISTORY RETROSPECTIVELY
OUR FUTURE BECOMES STANDSTILL EFFECTIVELY,

THE VERY PRESENCE OF SMALL PIECE OF TITBITS
MAKES OUR LIFE PRECIOUS AND
ADVENTUROUS JOURNEY TO DEAL WITH,

WITHOUT MUSE THERE IS NO NEWS
MUSE IS AN ACTION
WHEREAS NEWS IS OUR REACTION,

SO, WHAT'S IN NEWS?
OFFENDERS, CRIMINALS,
AN ACCUSED PERSON WILL ALWAYS REFUSE
THE HEINOUS CRIME TAKING PLACE
RISING ON IT'S TOLL LIKE A BIG MISHAP,

WE HOPE THE LADY-LUCK WOULD WORK
EVEN FOR SINNERS IF NOT MUCH

WITH THE FOOTAGE OF NEWS COVERAGE
OUR TENTACLES HAVE SPREAD ON IT'S OWN WAY
SO LET'S THINK, PONDER AND PROBE
EVERY POSSIBILITY IS EQUALLY THROWN,

BE IT BOLLYWOOD, POLITICAL, CRIMINAL OR ANY BEAT
NEWS HAS IT'S PLACE IN EVERY STORY ON IT'S SEAT,

THE ENTIRE WORLD HAS BECOME A GLOBAL-VILLAGE
AS WE KNOW VISIONARIES DON'T AGE,

NOW LET THE SPECULATORS SPECULATE
LEAVE IT TODAY!
TOMORROW WILL BE A NEW STORY,
WITH EVERY NOSTALGIC THOUGHT
YESTERDAY'S NEWS WAS BOUND
TO BE A PRESENT HISTORY,

REFLECTING OUR ACTION OF TODAY'S MAN
SLOWLY AND GRADUALLY OUR DAY WOULD END.

LOSING MY RELIGION.

LOSING MY RELIGION

WHEN HUMANITY APPEALS
AND RELIGION REVEALS
IT'S TRUE FORM OF
WHO I AM?
WHAT WE ARE?
WE DONT UNDERSTAND,

WHEN HISTORY REPEATS
WHATEVER IT'S EPIC DEPICTS
YOU FOLLOW WHAT IS
PREACHED INTO PRACTICE,

MAN MAKES A SIN
HE MAKES A CONFESSION
HE TRIES
TO RECEIVE SALVATION
BUT FALLS ASTRAY
AGAIN TO SEE WHAT
HEAVEN HAS
IN STORE FOR HIM
IN THE SKIES,

MY RELIGION IS MINE
WHO ARE YOU TO QUESTION?
I AM GOD OF MY OWN THOUGHT
LEAVE ME!
MY RELIGION IS MINE.

FOOTSTEPS ON THE SKY.

FOOTSTEPS ON THE SKY..

HERE I AM
CAUGHT UP IN THE SKY,
WITH CLOUDS
FLOATING AROUND ME
AND SUN RISEN,
WITH BRIGHT SHINING
BRAZEN LIGHT,

DEEP INSIDE
THE DARK NIGHT
WITH STARS SPARKLING
ENVELOPED ON THE BLACK SKY,

I AM GONE
AS YOU FORGONE
THE EXISTENCE OF
MY BODY AND SOUL,
ETERNALLY WITHOUT
PERPETUAL GOAL,

I VANISHED
LEAVING BEHIND
THE FOOTSTEPS
ON THE SKY,
AND THE SHOES I WORE
PERISHED
LEAVING YOU
WITH THE MEMORIES
ON THIS EARTH
SOLELY IT LIES.

A SWEET INTOXICATION.

A SWEET INTOXICATION

MY SOUL SMELLS SWEET
WHEN I AM INTOXICATED
WITH AN AROMA OF IT,

I PUFF AND SMOKE ALL MY
HEALTH'S WITNESS
NO TREASURE AND NO WEALTH
THAT I CAN HOLD FOR MY FITNESS,

I AFFIX THE THEORY OF INTOXICATION
ATTRIBUTING WEAKNESS OF ALL MY TENSION
EXCUSE ME PLEASE!
I SMOKE OUT OF MY
MIND'S OWN FRUSTRATION,

IT WOULD SERVE MY TEMPORAL PURPOSE
IF I QUIT MY SWEET INTOXICATION
I AM BACK TO MY LIFE'S
PERMANENT SOLUTION,

MY FRIENDS TOSS AROUND
"LET'S CHEERS!"
THE DEATH OF OUR LIFE,
WHEN MY FUNERAL WILL ARRRIVE
THEY WOULD APART FROM ME
FOR THE SEARCH OF
NEW FRIENDS INSTILLED WITH NEW LIFE.

AN UNANSWERED PRAYER.

AN UNANSWERED PRAYER

AN UNANSWERED PRAYER
ALWAYS GETS SILENTLY HEARD
NO MATTER EVEN IF YOU BLAST INTO TEARS,

NO MATTER WHERE YOU STAND
IN YOUR LIFE'S JOURNEY
YOUR PRAYERS WILL LAND
TILL YOUR DESTINY'S END,

WHETHER WE CRY OUT A RIVER OR
LOSE OUR FAITH ON LORD
THESE PRAYERS ARE REPLIED
WHEN HIS WILL COMES UPON,

PRAYERS NEVER GO UNHEARD
IN GOD'S NAME
WHETHER WE BLAME
BE IT FAITH OR FAME,

WHEN WE PRAY WITH FULL FAITH
OUR SPIRIT GETS ARISE
FROM THE ROOTS OF BELIEF
WHICH WE NEVER KEEP ASIDE,

BE IT ANY RELIGION
PRAYERS HAVE SCIENTIFIC REASONS,
TO REACH SPIRITUALISM
PRAYERS ARE THE ONLY SOLUTION.

FETCH MY THIRST.

FETCH MY THIRST..

OH! WATER
OH! WATER
I HAVE A LUST
FOR YOU TO COME HERE
AND FETCH MY THIRST,

FALL ON MY BODY
FEEL MY SOUL
DEPRIVED OF YOU
IN NATURES BOUNTY
I AM BESTOWED,

WITH YOU BEING
PURE AND SUBLIME
FEELING AS THOUGH
I HAVE REACHED UP IN THE SKY,

WASH MY PAIN
COME AND RAIN
WITH MY SORROWS
WHAT CAN I GAIN?

OH! WATER
OH! WATER
CLEAR ME
WITH DIRT
WHICH SHOULD NOT
LAST ON THIS EARTH,
OF FINEST PLEASURE
YOU HAVE OCCURRED.

AN ETERNAL TIME.

TIME WHICH IS TEMPORAL
IS NOT AT ITS ETERNITY,
TIME WHICH IS ETERNAL
IS A TIME
WHICH REMAINS PERMANENTLY,

TIME TELLS AND
TIME MAKES YOU AWAIT,
WHEN THERE IS NO MOVEMENT
THERE ISN'T ANY TIME,

WHEN THERE IS NO TIME
THE ACTION ON THIS EARTH
DOES NOT TAKES PLACE,
THE ACTION CREATES REACTION
IT RETALIATES,
BUT IT IS IN TIME
FOR AN ACTION TO REACT,

ACTION REPEATS AND
WORD REPEATS
BUT IN ETERNITY OF TIME
YOU SHALL NOT GET DEFEAT,

TIME IN ETERNAL
IS A TIME PERMANENT
WHILE TIME IS NOT SHORT-LIVED
LIFE HERE IS NOT PERCEIVED
TO BE A MAKE-BELIEVE,

WHEN TIME ETERNAL IS NOT PRESENT
THEN IN THAT TIME
WE ARE LEFT
PERMANENTLY IN IT'S ABSENCE.

IMMACULATE LOVE.

MY IMMACULATE LOVE EXIST
AS LORD'S MERCY AND PITY PERSIST,
WE ALL PRAY IN DAYS OF DISTRESS
WHEN WE ARE IN UTTER MOST DESPAIR,

FOR LOVE TOWARDS MAN
OUR CREATOR
WHO CREATED US
WITH HIS INGENIOUS HANDS,

THE TAPESTRY OF
THE NATURES BEAUTY
IS CAPTURED
IN HIS OWN LAND,

MOUNTAINS, SEAS AND SAND
IT IS NOT A CREATION OF MAN,

MY IMMACULATE LOVE PERSIST
ETERNALLY TILL MY SOUL MAY EXIST,

FOR A BEAUTY OF
MAIDEN WHO IS
MAKEUPLESS
WEARING LACES
ON HER FROCK
WANDERING IN A DIVINE PALACE

WHERE LORD DWELLS UPON,
O LORD!
O LORD!
SHE CRIES
LIKE AN INFANT

WE STOOD UPON
AS HIS CHILD
WITH NO BOUNDARIES
OF HIS INNOCENCE
WITH DIVINE HEART
HE ALMOST STRIKES
IN OUR LIVES.

WAITING FOR SOMEONE TO ARRIVE.

WAITING FOR SOMEONE TO ARRIVE
WHEN HARD DAY PASSES BY
IT IS HARD TO HOLD THIS MOMENT
I NEVER KNOW HOW TO SURVIVE,

I FORGO MY LOVE
TO FORGET MY PAST
BUT IT IS ALL INEVITABLE
WHICH SHOULD NEVER LAST,

THOSE TEARS I SHED
IN COMPANIONSHIP FOR
WHOM I WAS MADE,
THOUGH LEFT QUITE UNEXPLAINED,

MY WORDS MIGHT BE
MARKED WITH MISINTERPRETATIONS
TO MAKE ME UNAWARE
OF WHAT IT COULD LEAD AS LIFE'S REAL LESSONS,

WHEN WILL HE ARRIVE AGAIN?
TO CHERISH MY PURE LOVE
AND TRYING TO MAKE ME UNDERSTAND

WHEN THERE IS NO HOPE LEFT
IN DOUBT I WAS UTMOST KEPT
TO GET BACK MY TRUE LOVE
IS NOT AT ALL FATE
I CAN AFFORD TO MAKE
IT IS NOT THAT EASY
JUST TO WATCH AND WAIT.

WHERE ARE WE LEADING OURSELVES?

WHERE ARE WE LEADING OURSELVES?

ARE WE RUNNING TO
LEAD OURSELVES AND
IN THE PICTURE OF LIFE
NOT IMAGINED OURSELVES?
IS OUR IMAGINATION
OUT OF PERCEPTION?
IS OUR LIFE
OUT OF WORLDLY TIES?
DO YOU KNOW
WHERE ARE WE LEADING OURSELVES?
ARE WE LAUGHING
TO MAKE OURSELVES HAPPY
AND ARE WE CRYING
TO SHED OUT OUR PAINFUL TEARS,
WHEN PEOPLE RUN HELTER-SKELTER
THEY DON'T KNOW FOR WHAT
HAVE THEY MADE THEIR
LIFE AS A RACE,
WHEN A PERSON IS CRYING
THE ONLY CURE & SOLUTION
LIES WITH OTHERS HAVING NO TIME
IS TO `CONSOLE`
BUT IS THAT CONSOLENCE
WORTH FORGETTING OUR SORROWS?
IT LEADS US NOWHERE
BUT ONLY TO A BIT OF COMFORTABLE ZONE,

OUR DETERMINATION GOES ON
AS PER OUR IMAGINATION
AND IMAGINATION SETS OUR DETERMINATION
WHICH LEADS TO REALITY OF LIFE,
WHEN THE CHILD RUNS FAST
HE LEADS NOWHERE
IT IS JUST HIS PLAYFULNESS
BUT WHEN WE RUN FAST
WE ARE LEADING OURSELVES TO FORTUNE & DISTRESSMENT
WHICH PLAYS UPON ITSELF,
PEOPLE SAY THIS
PEOPLE SAY THAT
BUT WHAT WE NEED TO HEAR IS
WHERE HAVE WE LEADED OURSELVES,
WHEN THE PERCEPTION MATTERS
TO WHERE HAVE WE IMAGINED OURSELVES,
RUN! RUN! RUN! IS THE MOTTO OF LIFE
LEAD! LEAD! LEAD! IS THE PURPOSE OF LIFE
WE PRAY TO GOD
GOD LEAD US SOMEWHERE,
THE PATH WE TAKE
THE PATH WE FOLLOW
DOES MATTERS YOU A LOT
AND IT COMES TO YOU RELEVANTLY
WHERE YOU HAVE LEADED YOURSELF
DID OUR IMAGINATION WORK OUT?
DID OUR PERCEPTION HELP?
ALL WE REALIZE
WHEN WE LEAD OURSELVES

JUST ASK YOURSELF
ARE WE AWARE
WHEN WE ARE RUNNING
OR LOST OUR SENSES
JUST TO LEAD
SOMEWHERE!

HOW FAR WE REACH WHEN WE END TILL SKY!

HAVE YOU GONE BEYOND
THE BLUE VEIL[SKY]
OR JUST LANDED ON EARTH
WITHOUT ANY FAIL?

ASK THOSE BIRDS
WHEN THEY DO FLY
DO THEY REALLY TOUCH THE SKY?
ASK THOSE FISHES
WHEN THEY SWIM
DO THEY REALLY
FEEL THE SHADOW OF SEA?

HAS ANYBODY SEEN
THE BOUNDARIES OF LIFE?
HAVE FREED THEMSELVES
IN THE BORDERLESS SKY?

HOW FAR DID THE BIRD FLY?
WE STRUGGLED
AT THE BOTTOM OF EARTH
AND GO BENEATH TO SEE
THE LIGHT [GRAVE]
AND ULTIMATELY SAW
THE DARKEST SKY,

HOW DO WE SEE THE MEANING OF LIFE?
WHEN THE DARK SKY IS OVER
DO WE SEARCH THE LIFE
OR IN THE MIDST OF LIFE
WE SEARCH THE SKY [DEATH]

IF WISHES HAD WINGS
HORSES WOULD FLY,
DID WE REACH
LEAVING OUR JOURNEY BEHIND?

HOW FAR AN ANGEL HELPED?

LIFE IS ENDOWED
WITH INVISIBLE FRIENDS
TO BORROW OUR SORROW
IS IN THEIR LAND,
THEY CAME TO US
WHEN OTHERS LEFT US IN A LURCH
AND AS A GOOD SAMARITAN
HEARD OUR PRAYERS IN THE CHURCH,

THE MOMENT WE CRIED "GOD HELP US"
WE FORGET
TO PRAY "GOD MAKE US HELP OTHERS"
WHEN WE RESORT TO GOD
HE RESCUES US WITH ANGELS
HE SENDS ALL HIS BLESSINGS
AND NEVER A CURSE
THE CURSE WE CALL
IS HIS "BLESSINGS IN DISGUISE",

SOMEONE CALLS UPON US TO GIVE US THE POWER
THEY ARE ARMY OF ALMIGHTY
ENDOWED WITH EQUALLY GOD-LIKE QUALITIES
THEY WOULD BLOW OUR BREATH AWAY
AND RE-CONSTRUCT OUR ENTIRE LIFE,
THE MIRACLE-MACHINE OF GOD
WORKING WITH THEM
IS MEANT FOR US
WITHOUT ANY FAIL,

WE FELT TOTALLY
PEACE OF SOUL
PURITY OF MIND
PATIENCE OF HEART
WHEN THEY ARRIVED,

WHEN THERE IS NO ONE AROUND
WE FAIL TO REALIZE
SOMEONE IS IN OUR SURROUND
AND WHEN WE VALUE THEM AS "ANGELS"
WE FEEL THEIR PRESENCE

HOW FAR AN ANGEL HELPED?
THEY HELPED US,
THE MOMENT WE
SAT DOWN SADLY
STRUGGLED MADLY
SURVIVED BADLY AND
START UP AGAIN
WITH THE WORLD GLADLY.

A MUSE OF MUSIC.

A MUSE OF MUSIC

PLEASE PLAY THE MUSIC
AND SET THE MUSE
MUSIC IS A MAN'S MUSE
A MAN IS WITH MUSE AND MUSIC,

HE SHALL MAKE THE MOUNTAINS MOVE
WHICH MAKES HIS MUSE AND MUSIC TRUE,

WHEN HE SETS HIS MUSE
THE SOUNDS OF MUSIC THRILLS HIM
TO THE EXTENT OF WHICH
IT CHILLS HIM,

THE SHOW MUST GO ON
NO MATTER WHAT
EVEN IF THE SPECTATORS ARE GONE,

MUSIC MAKES YOU CULMINATE MUSE
DO NOT GET DEFUSED,

MUSE SETS MUSIC MANNERFULLY
THE CELEBRATION OF SONGS ARE
CRAFTED CAREFULLY,

MUSE AND MUSIC
MYSTIFIES THE MYSTERY
WHICH LIES IN THE HISTORY,

FROM SLEEP TO IT'S WAKE
IT IS ALWAYS TO INSPIRE
THE CONSCIOUSNESS
OF OUR MAKE.

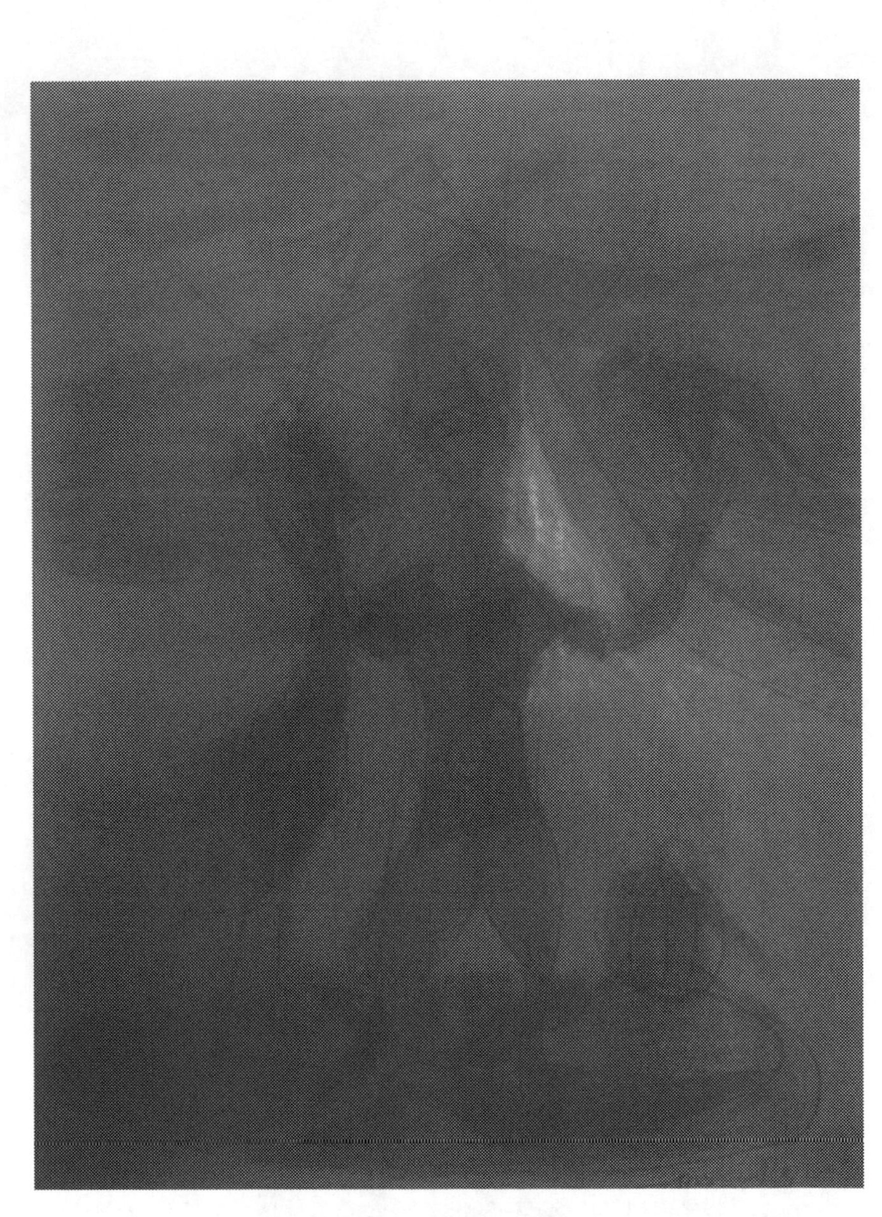

CARELESS WHISPER.

CARELESS WHISPER.

WHISPER CARELESSLY IN MY EARS
THOSE UNSOUND WORDS
WHICH I CANNOT HEAR,

WITH MEANINGLESS SPEECH
REACHING ME OVER A SOFT SILENCE,

THOSE SILENT MOMENTS REACHING WORDS
FORMING MEANINGS TO GET INTERPRETED
FOR YOU TO NOT GET FUMED AND FRETTED,

WORDS AFTER WORDS
WE SPEAK TO OURSELVES

WE WHISPER TO UTTER
WE RUSH TO PAUSE
WITH OR WITHOUT
A GOOD CAUSE,

WE SPEAK THIS
WE SPEAK THAT

AS WITHOUT CONVERSING
WE MAY FAIL
TO RELATE,

SO COME
LET'S COMMUNE
WITHOUT ANY FEAR
LEND ME YOUR EARS
GET HEARD!

NOVEMBER RAINS

OH RAIN! OH RAIN!
PLEASE COME
YOU ARE WELCOME
AND GO LIKE MY FRIEND

SET ME APART FROM SUN
DO NOT LET ME ANYMORE BURN,

GONE ARE THE DAYS
OF SUMMER SEASON
WHEN I SWEAT MY BROW
AND REAP HARVEST,

COME NOW!
COME NOW!
LAY ON ME AND HAVE A REST

KEEP ON FALLING
MAKE ME WET
SET ON ME NOW!
SET ON ME NOW!
WET.. WET.. WET..!!!

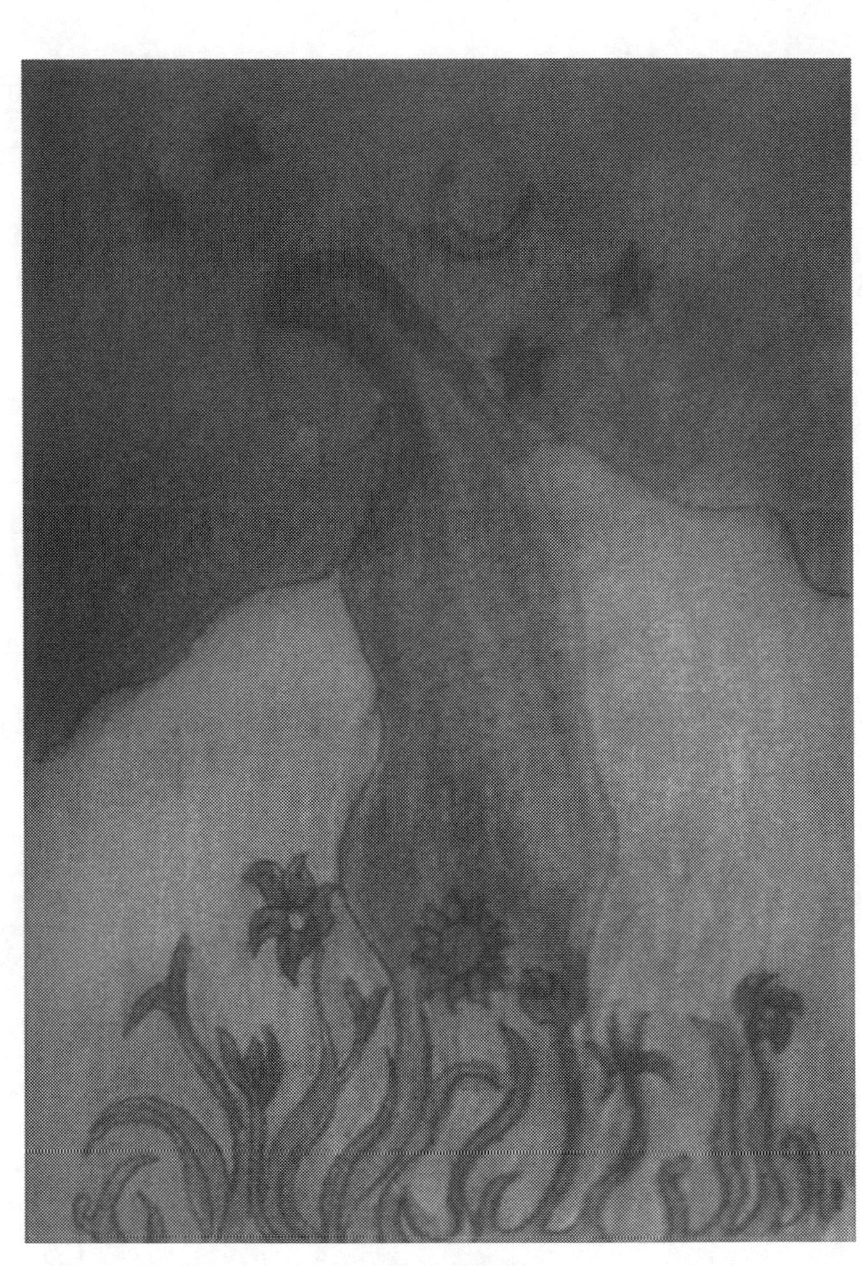

A SILENT FIGURE.

A SILENT FIGURE

IN MY FAR IMAGINATION
I SEE A NUDE FIGURE

MY NAKED EYE
TOUCHED THE FAR SIGHTED FEMALE FACE

DRESSED OF BEAUTIFUL FROCK AND
WITH TAPESTRY OF FABRIC LACE,

I CANNOT TAKE MY EYES OFF HER
AT THE VERY FIRST SIGHT
WHAT IT MUST BE
OH! MY LOVE
WHAT IT MIGHT?

AS I YEARN TO COME NEAR
SHE SHOWS HER WAY
TO GO FROM ME FAR AWAY

IT MAY NOT BE NOTICED BY HER
I AM A JILTED LOVER
THE LOVE WHICH
SHE CAN NEVER SHOWER,

AS I AM OF PASSIONATE
AND OF HEROIC KIND
MY FORESIGHT SEES HER
IN EVERY SIGHT OF MY MIND,

WISH TO KISS HER GOODBYE
AND BEFORE BADING HER BYE
LAST BUT NOT THE LEAST
MAY I HAVE THE WEDDING DONE
WITH HER ON A DAY OF HAPPY FEAST?

A HAPPY FAREWELL.

A HAPPY FAREWELL!!!

IT IS NOT AN EXIT LINE
TO ALWAYS BID GOODBYE
WITH A WARM AND
WELCOMING SMILE

WHEN YOU ARE LEFT ALOOF
AND FEEL ALONE
DON'T FORGET THAT
I AM HERE, NOT GONE

I WILL STAND BY YOU
I WILL SPEAK TO YOU
WORDS OF WISDOM
AND COURAGE TO SHOW,

SHOWER ME YOUR LOVE
PRAISE ME MY EXISTENCE
FOR YOU I HAVE COME
FOR YOU I AM GONE,

AS TO GET AWAY FROM YOUR LIFE
WAS DONE FOR YOUR FAVOUR
TO COMMIT MY PRESENCE
WAS DONE NEVER,

NOW THAT YOU SAID I AM GONE
LIKE STRANGERS WE MET
LIKE IN SAVAGE GARDEN
WE HAVE GROWN,

WE MET FOREVER
FOR THE VERY FIRST TIME
BUT MADE LOVE NEVER
TO REMEMBER LIFELONG.

GROW YOUNG, DIE INFANT!

WE ARE OLD ENOUGH
TO DIE YOUNG!
WHEN WE GROW YOUNG
WE DIE INFANT!

IN ALL OUR AGES WE EITHER HAVE LIFE
OR DEATH DESTINED BEFORE US!

WHEN WE ARE BORN
WE ARE YOUNGER INFANT,
AS A CHILD WE ARE INCLINED
AWAITING DEATH
FOR WHAT WE ARE MEANT,

WHEN WE GROW
WE GRADUALLY DIE OLD
SO GROW YOUNG AND
DIE INFANT!

LIFE IS A MYSTERY
DEATH IS A MIRACULOUS HISTORY
WHICH REPEATS ITSELF,
ONCE YOU ARE DONE
WITH YOUR LESSONS OF LIFE
DEATH TAKES IT'S SEAT
TO TEACH YOU WITH MORAL OF ALL KINDS,
IT CASTS YOU WITH MAGICAL SPELL OF AGES
WITH ALL DIFFERENT PHASES,

BID GOODBYE
TO DREADFUL DEATH
AND CHERISH AN UPCOMING LIFE
WELCOMING NEW LIFE,
WITH A WARM WITTY SMILE,

THIS IS ONLY ONE TIME CHANCE
YOU MAY NOT KNOW
WHAT YOU LOSE
WHAT YOU MIGHT HAVE WON,
OR ELSE?

JOIN THE CELEBRATION
OF MYSTIQUE CHARM
OF MYSTERIOUS LIFE
LEADED BY CHARISMA
OF YOUR OWN IDENTITY,

WHEN YOU REVEAL
YOUR PASS-LIVED LIFE
OF YOUR OWN AGE
YOU REALIZE
MORE OR LESS,

YOU MAY FACE
THE JOURNEY
OF HEAVENLY ABODE
DESTINED HERE,
NEITHER PRE-PLANNED
NOR FORESEEN YET,
LEAVING YOU APART
FROM ALL HUMANLY STRIFE.

AN ECHO OF UNNOTICED FOOTSTEPS.

AN ECHO OF UNNOTICED FOOTSTEPS

AN UNNOTICED ECHO
RESOUNDS AT YOUR DOOR
AT EVERY NOOK AND CORNER OF
WHERE YOU DWELL TO GO,
YOU CAN'T REASON OUT
WITH UTMOST CARE
YOU CAN'T FIGURE OUT
WHY WAS IT LEFT
UNNOTICED, UNDONE AND UNFAIR,

AN ECHO THAT RINGS;
THIS SILENT SOUND
MAKES YOU THINK
THAT WHAT YOU SPEAK
KEEPS ITSELF RESOUND IN AIR,

A WONDERFUL CORNER
FOR ECHO TO ENJOY
AND BE DELIGHT
IS WHEN YOU STAY SILENTLY
AT YOUR VERY OWN SIGHT,

WITHOUT YOUR CAREFUL PRESENCE
ECHOES DON'T EXIST
IT IS A MERE NOISY REFLECTION
OF VOCAL CHORDS WHICH NEVER RESIST
MAKING STUNNED AND STIRRED
THOSE SCARCELY AUDIBLE PERFORMANCE,

ECHO IS A SOUND

OF YOUR OWN VOICE REFLECTION

IT IS YOUR CALL TO HEAR

WHICH PLEASES YOUR EARS,

THE SOUNDS OF SORROWFULNESS

WITH THE HAPPY INFLUENCE

THE ECHOES OF LIFE

WHICH CARRIES IT'S SOUND

FOR YEARS AND YEARS

KEEPING YOU UNNOTICED

OF THE AGE YOU BEAR.

DEVIL'S DELIGHT

IN THE MIDDLE OF NIGHT
WHEN SPIRITS ARISE
YOU TEND TO FEEL SPOOKY
AND GET YOURSELF AWAKEND
WITH SCARRY THOUGHT OF WHAT IT MIGHT?

BUT THE GHOST WITHIN YOU
WHICH YOU CARRY
HOW CAN YOU GET RID
OF THAT INNERSIGHT?

THE BEAUTY IN THE BEAST
THE BEAUTY OF THE BEAST
LIES IN THE BEHOLDER'S SIGHT

IT MAY SEEM THAT IT IS ALL RIGHT,
A BEAUTIFUL BODY
AND IT'S SENSUOUS APPEAL
THAT WITH IT'S BEAUTY
IT MAY FEEL DELIGHT,

WITH IT'S REFLECTION
AND IT'S REVEALATION

WHEN IT'S LOVER
CAN DISCOVER
HE WILL NEVER
BE LEFT UNSATISFIED
AND WILL BE SURE
THAT IT IS THE REAL DEVIL'S DELIGHT
WHICH COMES AGAINST DIVINE LIGHT.

NO PROBLEM

WHEN LIFE PERSISTS
YOU CEASE TO EXIST,

YOUR EXISTENCE SERVES
A MERE SOLITARINESS
TO FIND A REFLECTION
OF YOUR MIRROR IMAGE,

WHETHER YOU LIVE OR DIE
YOU TEND TO BEGIN
LIKE AN INFANT'S SORROWFUL CRY

PLEASE! HELP ME OUT....
AND YOU FIND NONE TO RESORT,

WITHOUT YOU PERMITTING
A PROBLEM TO EXIST
THE SOLUTION TOWARDS IT
WILL NEVER ARISE

AS BEFORE WE PERISH,
PROBLEMS ARE MANY
SINCE OUR DAYS OF LIFE,

IT IS A CHILD'S PLAY
MADE LIKE A SAND OF CLAY,

WHEN WE TRY TO RESOLVE
IT GETS MORE AND MORE
COME ON...!

LET'S SOLVE OUR PLOBLEM
WHEN THE SOUL DEPARTS
FROM OUR BODY
OUR PROBLEMS GET
[RE]SOLVED MIRACULOUSLY!

A MOONY DAY!

AS THE SEASHORE
WITH THE STILLED WATER
REMAINS MOTIONLESS
REACHING TO STAGNATE,

WHEN THE SUN SETS DOWN
ARISING TWILIGHT WITH GOLDEN RAYS,
WE SEE DARKNESS COMING ALL AROUND

THE ROMANCE SETS IN
AS THE LOVERS PASS BY THOSE
SAVAGE GARDENS
THROUGH SOFT PETALS OF ROSE,

THE LOVER CARESSES AND CUDDLES
HE LOVES BELOVED OUT OF PASSION
AND NOT TO LET GO
SUCH LIMITS OF EMOTIONS,

FOR HE IS TRULY MOONY
TO MAKE PURE LOVE
TO HIS BELOVED SO DEEPLY,

HIS SENSUOUS APPEALS
TO HIM SO LOVELY
THAT HIS IMAGERY OBSERVES
TAPESTRY OF HER BEAUTY,

THIS THE DARK FIGURE OF HIS LOVE
APPEARS TO HIM WHEN
MOON ENLIGHTENS
IT'S SILVER RAYS;
IT BRIGHTENS HIS LOVE MORE AND MORE
LIKE A SPARK OF FIRE OF SUNNY RAYS,

FROM DARKNESS TO DAYLIGHT
THE PASSION OF LOVE
AMOUNTS LOVERS TO ARISE.

TEARS OF JOY.

TEARS OF JOY

MISSING YOU SO MUCH
JUST TEARS UPON MY HEART
THAT I HATE TO SEE US APART,
WALKING AROUND THE BUSH
TRYING TO FIND THE ROOF,

FOLLOWING ENTIRE DAYS OF TEARS
TAKING A SIP
DRINKING A COLD BEER
I WAS MISSING YOU SO MUCH
THAT YOU WERE HERE,

I REALIZED THAT I FEEL
THOSE SENSES LEFT BEHIND
THAT YOU WILL ALWAYS BE MINE
WITH VAGUE AND VIVID
MEMORIES OF MY MIND,

WALKING ALL ALONE ON THE STREET
THINKING THAT YOU LOVE ME SO DEEP
TO BELIEVE OR NOT
YOU ARE THE ONE I WANT
JUST STARRING AT YOUR EYES
WISHING TO BE WITH YOU
WITH REST OF MY LIFE.

IF I LOSE YOU

YOU SAY YOU KNOW ME
MORE THAN MY OWN IMAGE DOES,
MY MIRROR LIES
WHILE LISTENING THOSE CRIES,

I LOST YOU AT THE COST OF
YOUR INNOCENCE
WHAT WAS MY PRETENCE
WITH YOUR LOVE?
WHAT WAS MY LUST?

I AM CRYING OUT A RIVER
IS THERE ANYONE TO HEAR?
THOSE TEARS OF SADNESS
THOSE DAYS OF MADNESS,

MY LOVE WAS OUT OF PASSION
YOU ARE MY BETRAYAL
YOU TAUGHT ME BETTER
A BITTER LESSON,

LOVE ME OR NOT
I NEED NOT WANT
NEEDLESS HOPE
THIS PAINFUL LIFE
I HAVE GOT,

WHO AM I TO REFUSE?
FOR YOU TO MAKE ME LOSE
YOU ONLY HAD TO CHOOSE.

AWAITING FOR LOVE

THESE DAYS HAVE PASSED AWAY AND GONE
OUR WAYS OF BEING TOGETHER
HAVE BEEN ALMOST FORGONE,

NO MORE TREES
TO WITNESS
OUR KISS,

NO MORE DREAMS
TO VISION
OUR SIGHT

WHEN I AM ALONE
LEFT ALOOF
IF YOUR MEMORIES WILL PREVAIL
UNDER THIS ONE ROOF,

YOU HAD COME HOME
YOU HAD GONE
GIVING ME COURAGE
TO BID YOU BYE,
AWAITING FOR YOUR LOVE
TO STAY AWAY
AND MOURN MYSELF TO DIE.

TO MARRY A MAN?

I AM GOING TO MARRY A MAN
THOUSANDS AND MILLIONS
ON THIS LAND!

WHOM DO I MARRY?
WITH WHOM SHALL I CARRY
AN INTENSE AFFAIR?

I THOUGHT TO MYSELF
THERE IS NO ONE
IN THE CROWDED LIFE'S
CRAZY GAME
BUT SOON REALISED
WHEN I SAW
WHAT I CLAIM,

A MAN WITH
DOZEN ROSES
A MAN WITH
THOUSAND KISSES,

EVERYDAY WHEN I APPEAR
FROM MY SOUNDED SLEEP
I SHOULD KNOW
I DREAMT
ONLY OF HIM,

SWEET MEMORIES
MAY NOT TURN
INTO TRAGEDIES
OF THIS LIFE,

I PRAY EVERYDAY
I MARRY A MAN
WHO WILL
HAVE FOR ME
INFINITELY A GREAT RESPECT
INTENSED WITH LOVE
UTMOST WITH CARE.

A FREE BONDAGE.

A FREE BONDAGE

FREEDOM FREEDOM
I FOLLOW THAT!
TO ME
I AM SLAVE TO MYSELF,

WHEN I WAS SET FREE
I SEEK TO SEARCH LIFE
AS A CAGED HUMAN
THEN I CREID
FREEDOM! FREEDOM!
I FOLLOW THAT!

WHEN I AM FREED
WITH NO BONDAGE
I SEARCH DEATH
IN THE MIDST OF MY LIFE,

AS A DYING HUMAN
I PUT REST TO MY SOUL
THEN I SHOUTED
WITH MY SUBDUED VOICE
TO MAKE A CALL
FREEDOM! FREEDOM!
I FOLLOW THAT!

FREE FROM WHAT?
FREE FROM WHERE?

IN THE SHADOW OF NIGHT
PREVAILS DAYLIGHT,

WITHIN THE PRISON OF GOLDEN RODS
I AM JUST A SOBBING SOUL,

DEPRIVED OF NATURAL BOUNTIES
WHICH ARE BESTOWED BY GOD
ONLY FOR ME,

OUT OF SLAVERY
WITH BONDAGE
FREEDOM! FREEDOM!
I FOLLOW THAT!

ALIENS IN THE WONDERLAND.

ALIENS IN THE WONDERLAND!

WE CALL THEM ALIENS
WHEREAS WE ARE UNKNOWN TO OURSELVES,
THIS STRANGE FEELING OF TOGETHERNESS
THIS ECCENTRIC WAYS OF LONELINESS,
EMOTIONALLY BOUNDED
SPIRITUALLY WOUNDED
AS SUCH WE ARE
ALIENS IN THE WONDERLAND!

THIS WORLD HAS TURNED
INTO A "GLOBAL-VILLAGE"
WHERE THE NECESSITY
OF OUR NEARBY NEIGHBOURS
LIES IN SCARCITY
AS SUCH WE ARE
ALIENS IN THE WONDERLAND!

WHERE DO WE COME FROM?
WHERE DO WE GO?
WE ARE KNOWN AS
HUMANLY CREATURES
WE ARE VANISHED
FAR AWAY FROM COSMOS
MAY BE IN OTHER LAND
AS SUCH WE ARE
ALIENS IN THE WONDERLAND!

FADES AWAY.

FADES AWAY

THE DAY AND NIGHT
GOES ON WITH OUR HOPE OF LIGHT
THE MEMORIES OF IT WHICH PREVAILS
PERSISTS WITH US
TILL WE EXIST ON THIS EARTH,

AS A SOUL NEVER FAILS
IT'S BODY
TO GET FADE AWAY,

WHEN THE LOVER HOLDS HIS BELOVED
HE INTERNALLY DRIFTS
TO EXPRESS HIS LOVE
IN MANY WAYS,

GOD HAS MADE
INGENIOUSLY WITH HIS OWN HANDS
ALL HUMAN CREATURES
WHO PERISH AND
FADES AWAY,

WE GAZE AT THE STARS
ON THE DARK ENVELOPED SKY
BUT THE BLINKING STAR
SPARKLING FOR AWHILE
SOOTHING TO SET ENTIRE NIGHT SOON
FADES AWAY,

WE SEE FLOWERS BLOOMING
IN THE ORCHID
IN MANY COLORS
GREETING YOU EARLY MORNING
TO STAY AWAKE
BUT AS SOON AS BRIGHT SUNLIGHT ARISES
THOSE FRAGNANCES OF FRESH FLOWERS
FADES AWAY,

PEOPLE OF DIFFERENT AGES
FROM INFANCY TO THEIR AGED DAYS
PASS AWAY THEIR LIFE
ON THIS TEMPORAL WORLD
GETTING VANISHED AND
MERGING WITH THE BLUE SKY
GETTING THEMSELVES DIE
FADES AWAY.

IT IS ALL ALONE

IN MY SOLITARINESS
LIES MY COMPANIONSHIP,

CLUBBED BY THIS CROWD
I FEEL ALOOF,

MY SOUL SOLELY ASKS
WHO AM I
TO BELONG?

MY MIRROR REFLECTS
THE IMAGE OF WHICH
I CANNOT MAKE,

ALONE ON THIS
COSMIC WORLD,
DO I KNOW
ANY HUMAN LIKE ME
ON THIS EARTH?

SLEEPING CHILD

OH! MY SLEEPING CHILD
I WANT TO SING FOR YOU
A SWEET LULLABY,

WHEN THE WORLD GROWS WILD
YOU ACT LIKE A CHILD,

YOUR INNOCENCE IS A BLISS
YOUR HAPPINESS IS IN PEACE,

YOU ARE ESTRANGED
FROM THE MATERIALISTIC WORLD
YOU ARE THE TREASURE
OF OUR CREATOR,

DREAMS OF THIS WORLD
MAY COME TRUE FOR YOU,
NO NIGHTMARES
I WISH FOR YOU.

A LUNATIC WORLD.

A LUNATIC WORLD!!!

A LUNATIC WORLD!
A LUNATIC WORLD!
TRIES
AFTER EVERY LAUGHTER
IT CRIES
THE WORRIES SET
IN THEIR MINDS,

NO MONEY
NO TIME

THE CROWD MOVES
GETS CLUBBED
IN THE DISCO
OF MADNESS
OF THIS ENTIRE WORLD,

THEY DANCE THE RHYTHM
OF SONG
IN INSANE MANNER,

THEY MOURN
THE PAIN OF SORROWS,
THAT THEY FEEL,
DEEP INSIDE
THEY RESIST
FROM LAUGHTER'S CRY
WHICH THEY CAN NOT REVEAL.

WALK OF LIFE.

WALK, THE WALK OF LIFE
LIKE A STRAIGHT PATH
YOUR ROAD SHOULD ARISE,

IN DESTINY
TO SURVIVE
YOU SHOULD
AVOID ANY WAYS
CAUSING STRIFE,

BUT CONFLICTS ARE
THE WAYS OF LIFE
ON THIS EARTH
AS TO DEAL
WITH SUCH
YOU SHOULD
HAVE VITAL STRENGTH
AND CLEAR CONSCIENCE,

DON'T GET EMOTIONALLY SLAYED
WALK, THE WALK OF YOUR LIFE
THE WAY LORD HAS MADE
THE ROAD OF YOUR EACH DAY
MOULDS YOUR BODY
JUST LIKE THAT OF CLAY,

STRAIGHTEN YOUR PATH
REACH THE POINT
WHERE YOU SEE
HEAVEN ON EARTH.
HOPE NOT THE HELL!
TO FALL UPON,

CAUSE IT MAY
LEAD YOU TO
THE WRATH OF LORD
AND MAKE YOU BURN,

AS THIS LIFE HAS
NO TURNING POINT
DEATH IS YOUR DESTINY
AND AFTER YOUR BIRTH
ONLY YOU WERE ANOINT.

AN EVERLASTING SILENCE.

AN EVERLASTING SILENCE REVEALS
WORDS WHICH COULD NOT GET REPEAT,

AFTER EVERY SPEECH
IT REACHES SOME POINT OF SILENCE
WHICH IT TRIES TO SEEK
IN THE MATTER OF COMMUNICATION
IT IMPERSONALLY GETS DEFEAT,

WORDS AFTER WORDS
FORM A SOCIAL WORLD
FOR A HUMAN TO REACT
WHERE LANGUAGES ARE SIGNED
IN THE WAY OF POLITICAL PACT
WE ARE HERE TO SPEAK AND ACT.

IN THE DARKEST SHADOW

HERE WE GO
TO FOLLOW
THE DARKNESS OF GRAVE
FOR THE LIFE WE CRAVE

IN THE DARK NIGHT PREVAILS
THE SHADOW WHICH ALMOST
REMAINS IN VEIL,

THIS STRANGE FIGURE APPEARS
IN MY VIVID MEMORY
EVERY DAY AND NIGHT,

IT SHOWS ME THE PATH
WHERE NONE COULD LAST,

AND DISAPPEARS IN IT'S MYSTERIOUS WAYS
HOPING TO SHOW IT'S PRESENCE IN SUN'S RAYS.

TIME OF LIFE:

LIFE IS SHORT AND
TEMPORAL TO BE,
WHY DON'T YOU
BELONG TO ME?

YOU SAY
"BE WITH ME FOR A MOMENT"
BUT MY WHOLE LIFE
GETS SEIZED
IN EXISTENCE
OF YOUR SOLITARINESS,

OF WHAT VALUE
DO I ACCORD TO YOU,
OH! MY LOVER?

WHEN MY LIFE ITSELF
WON'T BE IN PRESENCE,

YOU SAY,
"IT IS A PART OF LIFE
DEALING WITH NO PERMANENCE",
BUT I WAS THERE FOR A MINUTE
OF YOUR TIME, SPACE OR DISTANCE,

SHALL I SAY,
MY HEART WAS TORNED APART
TO YEARN FOR YOUR PRESENCE
IN ETERNAL AND ACHIEVE YOU
OVEREACHING YOUR EMOTIONS?

SPIRITUAL WISDOM.

THE SPIRITUAL WISDOM

IN MY SPIRITS
I ACHIEVE MY ETERNITY
TO SEARCH GREAT FREEDOM
BONDED TO SLAVERY,

WHEN THE WORLD SEIZES TO EXIST
MY SPIRITUAL WISDOM
CAN NOT RESIST,

TO FEEL THE PAIN
WHICH I CAN'T FEEL
TO SEEK THE WORLD
WHERE I CAN'T REACH,

THE SALVATION WHICH I SEEK TO SEARCH
THE ROOM TO WORDLY WISDOM IS AS SUCH
FOR WHICH I LOST AN UTMOST URGE.

SUICIDE OF MY LIFE.

SUICIDE OF MY LIFE.

I HAVE SUBMITTED
MY LIFE TOWARDS
LORD'S DEVOTION,
WITH THIS TENDENCY
I HAD SUCH EMOTIONS,

MY IMMACULATE LOVE
TO MEET MY LORD
MADE ME
DO SUICIDE OF MY LIFE,
WITH SUCH
SINFUL THOUGHT
I HAD TO SURVIVE,

AS I MERGE
WITH THE BLUE SKY
THERE MAY BE RENEWAL
OF MY PRESENT LIFE,
KEEPING THIS FORLORN HOPE
I ENDED MY LIFE
ON THIS EARTH,

BUT LORD TOLD ME
TO LIVE TILL I DIE
A NATURAL DEATH
AS TO GIVE ME BIRTH
HE MAY NOT REGRET.

IN MY DESTINY THERE IS NO END.

IN MY DESTINY THERE IS NO END.

THIS THE JOURNEY OF LIFE
WHERE THERE IS A BEGINNING
WHERE THERE LIES ENDLESS
ADVENTURES TO CREATE,

DESTINY IS ETERNAL
AND IN IT'S ETERNITY
THERE IS NO END,

LIVING LIFE DEADLY ALIVE
IN OUR BIRTH
WE ARE BORN TO DEATH,

THE PLACE OF OUR GRAVE
WHERE WE DWELL
FOR OUR LIFE TO CRAVE,

WHERE DO WE COME FROM?
WHERE DO WE NEED TO GO?

WE CEASE TO EXIST
IN WORDLY AFFAIRS,
TO GAIN SPIRITUAL WISDOM
FULL OF ITS RICHNESS,

THIS THE MAN OF THE MATERIAL WORLD
THIS THE MOTHER NATURE AND MY CREATOR;
IN MY DESTINY
THERE IS NO END

AS WE CEASE TO EXIST

OUR SOUL

CRIED IN PAIN,

NOT MUCH TO LOOSE

NOT MUCH TO GAIN

IN MY DESTINY

THERE IS NO END!!!

YES BOSS...

I SALUTE YOU SIR
FROM TOP OF MY HAT
TILL BOTTOM OF MY HEART
I SWEAR
YES BOSS
WHATEVER YOU SAY..
I DO CARE,

IT IS SAID AND DONE
IRRESPECTTIVE OF
WHAT YOU THINK
RIGHT OR WRONG
AFFECTING EVERYONE
OR SAY NONE
I SWEAR
I DO CARE,

WHEN YOUR BOSS FIRES YOU
AT THE TOP OF HIS VOICE
YOU GET SUBMISSIVE
WITH THE ACT OF HIS NOISE
I SWEAR
I DO CARE,

I GRUDGE AND ENVY
THE POSITION YOU CARRY
ASKING TO FACE CHALLENGES
AND THE RESPONSIBILITIES

WHICH YOU CARRY;
I WISH I WAS YOU
AND YOU MY SLAVE
I WOULD MAKE YOU
TORTURE AND TAUNT,
BUT, WHEN I BE BOSS
I WOULD MISS
WHAT YOU TAUGHT
AS TRYING TO LEARN FROM OTHERS
WOULD NOT BE A GOOD JOB
I SWEAR
I DO CARE,

THE WISH TO FULLFILL
THE TOP CORPORATE POSITION
OF OUR ORGANISATION'S NEEDS
CARRIES ALOT OF FRUSTRATION
IT IS NO MORE THAN KILLING HUNGER
FOR OUR OWN HUMANLY GROWTH
AS IT INDIRECTLY SECURES
THE NEED OF OUR NATION
WHO PAYS HEAVY TAXES
AND PAVES WAY TO THE MINISTER'S POCKETS,
SO
NATION, NATION
I SHOUT THE INDIAN SLOGAN
"*VANDEY MAATARAM*"
YES BOSS
IT LITERALLY
MAKES A BEELINE
TO "*KHISA-KATARAM*" (POCKET-PINCHING).

BOLLYWOOD BIZ!!!

IT IS A GREAT BOLLYWOOD BIZ!

RIGHT FROM IMRAN HASHMI'S
LAST WISH
TO SPRAY DEO
AND MAKE A KISS,

FROM SALMAN KHAN'S
ENERGY AND STRENGTH
TO MAKE "REVITAL" GAIN,

PRIYANKA'S BRAND NEW "SCOOTY"
MAKES HER
TURN HER CAREER
TO TAKE FOR A RIDE
BOLLOYWOOD'S BITCH FIGHT,

KATRINA'S SMART PHONE "SONY"
SOUNDS SO PHONEY,

RANBIR'S "LENOVO" LAPTOP
IS AN AD WHICH TURNS HIM INTO
BIGTIME FILM-FLOP,

BIG B'S KALYAN JEWELLERS
MAKES SURE YOU SHINE
LIKE HIM IN A SPOT LIGHT
OF PURE GOLDEN GOLD MINE,

WHILE THIS AD IS A GOOD ENTERTAINING FACTOR

WE ALL ARE POOR PAYING SPECTATORS

AND AT THE COST OF ACTORS TO ACT

WE JUST PUBLICLY

STAND STOICAL

TO REACT

CLAP! CLAP! CLAP!

MY BELOVED EXIST.

ON MY CORPSE
BELOVED CRIED
IF YOU DO NOT LOVE ME
I WILL DIE,

OH! COME HERE
LOVE ME ETERNALLY
WAS MY EMOTIONAL OUTCRY,

SEIZE THIS MOMENT
IN TEMPORAL TIMES,

BRING MY BODY
TO MY BELOVED
BEFORE MY SOUL FLIES.

PERSONAL-PEOPLE.

THIS THE TENDENCY
OF A HUMAN PSYCHOLOGY,
TO SEE OTHER'S WEAKNESSES
AS THEIR OWN STRONG POINT,
IN THIS SPIRITUAL WORLD
THEY SEEK TO SEARCH
BUT FAIL TO SERVE
A TRUE SOCIAL LIFE
THEY JOINED,

OF WHAT IS DESTINED
IS GOING TO HAPPEN,
OF CROWDED PEOPLE
CLADED WITH VEIL,
WE FAIL TO SEE
WHAT OUR VISION
SAYS TO BE...

ENJOYING ENTERTAINMENT
GETTING REGALED AT,
WE ARE ALL STUCK
WITH DAILY DANCE
TO WORK AND FORGET.

A POETICAL NOTE.

A POETICAL NOTE

IN MY SOLITARY GRIEF
LIES YOUR MEMORIES,
AS DAY AND NIGHT
ALWAYS ARISE
MY SUN SET,
ONLY WHEN YOU LEFT,

POETICAL LINES JUST FOR YOU......
I KEPT WRITING
KEEPING YOU IN MY MIND
BUT, IN MY VIVID MEMORIES
YOU NEVER FADED
BEING SO ALIVE,

WHEN DAY ARRIVES
TO BADE GOODBYE
TO DARKEN THE LIGHT,
I ALMOST MISS
TO SEE YOU
BY MY SIGHT,
I AM WAITING
FOR GOOD TIME
THOUGH IT PASSES BY,
I NEVER WANT
TO LET YOU GO
EVEN IF YOU
MAKE ME CRY,

THIS THE SONG I HEAR
THIS DANCE I REGALED AT
IS MY LIFE SO PRECIOUS
FOR THE MOMENTS
I NEED TO CELEBRATE?

JUST CHERISH THE DREAMS
WISHING YOU WERE WITH ME,
THEN PAUSE AND PONDER
WHAT MIGHT?
WHAT MIGHT NOT BE?

THE DAY YOU CAME TO ME
I DIDN'T FEEL A MIRACLE STRUCK,
BUT HEAVENS FALL FOR ME
WHEN YOU GAVE YOURSELF TO ME,

THIS THE TENDENCY
TO END UP MY LIFE
HAS MADE ME SO MUCH ALIVE,
I AM DEADLY LIVING
TO MYSELF THIS MOMENTS
AS THEY LIVE BY,

MY MEMORIES
GETS MESMERISED
WITH THE IMPACT
OF YOUR THOUGHT,
STANDING UNDER THE DARK SKY
WHERE MILLIONS OF INFINITE STARS
MAKE ME LOST,

THIS THE VACCUM
OF MY EMPTY LIFE
HAS NO MEANINGFUL PURPOSE TO SERVE,
WANDERING ADRIFT ON THE PATH
WHERE CHILDREN PLAY ON THE PARK,

YOU CHOSE ME
NOT TO FREE YOURSELF
UNLESS OUR RELATION
GETS SOLEMNIZED
INTO A DIVINE MARRIAGE,

IT WAS UNEXPECTED
YET FOR A SITUATION
TO COME
OF YOU AND ME
WITH HURDLES APART FROM IT,
I PROBABLY ASKED YOU A WRONG QUESTION
"WILL YOU MARRY ME?"
THOUGH I WILL KEEP
HOLD ON YOU AND WAIT
TO SEE AHEAD
WHAT'S NEXT
LEFT UNEXPECTED,

THE DAY YOU MAKE ME ASSURED
I WOULD SURRENDER MY SOUL,
WHEN MY HEART HURTS
TO SEE YOU SO STILL AND COLD
I GO ON WITH MY LIFE
IN SOLITARY TO HOLD,

WHEN YOU ARE NOT BONDED
IF I GIVE YOU MY HEART INDEED,
ON WHAT ACCOUNT DO I SEE THE WORLD
WITH YOUR EYES TO BE SEEN?

I REMEMBER THOSE DAYS
WHEN YOU TOOK ME
INTO YOUR ARMS
CUDDLING AND CARESSING ME,
I REMEMBER THOSE PLEASURABLE MOMENTS
WHEN YOU PLANTED
A LOVELY KISS
ON MY CHEEKS,

I FORGO MY DREAMS
WHEN YOU CAME INTO REALITY
OF MY FICTITIUOS LIFE,
AS I TEND TO FORGET
ALL THE FACTS,
WHEN YOUR IMAGE
WAS CREATED
IN THE PICTURE
OF MY LIFE,

THESE DAYS HAVE GONE
AS MY HOPES HAVE TURNED
INTO A FORLORN-HOPE,
AS DAY BY DAY
PASSES BY,
I GET EAGER TO REMEMBER
WHAT NEXT LIES,

WISHING YOU WERE HERE
IN MY SOLITARINESS
I DO CONFESS!

HERE I END
WITH A POETICAL NOTE
MY LITTLE WORDS SAYS THAT...
THIS IS ALL BY GRACE OF GOD!
THAT I AM ABLE TO VENT OUT
MY HEAVY HEART
WITH TEARS SET APART,

THE DARK NIGHT HAS COVERED
MY FACE FORTUNATELY
AS BRIGHTENED STARS
SMILE AT ME
WHILE I SOB
IN A MYSTERY,
WRITING ON A PIECE OF PAPER
A PASSIONATE POETRY...........

Author: SAMINA SAIFEE.